T0343613

Animal logo

Counter–Print Books

Contents

Foreword

Animal Logo was the first in a series of six books that originally came out in 2008. We were initially drawn to animal logos, as a subject matter, as they seemed to contain a warmth and personality missing in other marks of identity. On the book's tenth anniversary, we revisited the theme and expanded and updated the collection to form this casebound edition.

Ten years on, animal logos are still as ubiquitous in modern branding, with companies ranging from sports teams to multinational corporations using these images to connect with consumers. But what is it about animal logos that make them so powerful and effective?

Throughout history, animals have played an important role in human culture and mythology, serving as symbols of power, wisdom and instinct. From the lion of the ancient Greeks to the Chinese dragon, animals have been used to represent everything from national identity to personal characteristics. Today, animal logos continue this tradition, communicating a range of messages to consumers.

One of the most important functions of animal logos is to convey a sense of identity and personality. By associating themselves with a particular animal, a company can convey a sense of strength, agility, or cunning, depending on the animal chosen. For example, a sports team might choose a fierce predator like a tiger or a panther to convey a sense of strength and ferocity, while a company that values intelligence and adaptability might choose a fox or a dolphin as its logo.

Another important function of animal logos is to evoke emotions and associations in consumers. Research has shown that people have deep-seated emotional connections to certain animals, based on cultural associations and personal experiences. By using an animal logo, a company can tap into these emotional connections, creating a sense of affinity and loyalty among consumers.

The design of an animal logo is a complex process that involves careful consideration of the animal's anatomy, behavior and cultural associations, as well as the specific needs of the brand. A well–designed animal logo should be both instantly recognisable and visually appealing, while also conveying a clear message about the brand's identity and values.

In this book, you will see the different design strategies used to create effective animal logos, from the use of stylized silhouettes to the incorporation of logotypes and minimalism via the reduction of form.

Whether you are a designer looking to create a memorable animal logo for a client, a marketer seeking to understand the power of animal logos in branding, or simply a curious consumer interested in branding, this book has something to offer. So come along on this extended journey of discovery and explore the fascinating world of animal logos.

Jon Dowling
Counter–Print

Aquatic

Ely & District CAMRA
Campaign for real ale

Maddison Graphic
maddisongraphic.com
United Kingdom
2010

Amar Caribe
Natural water

Enrike Puerto
enrikepuerto.com
Mexico
2020

Johan Broman
Sport fishing equipment

Redmanwalking
redmanwalking.com
Sweden
2005

Mapexel
Food

Oscar de Castro
oscardecastro.com
Spain
2012

A.D.Deertz
Menswear

123buero
123buero.com
Germany
2006

Thinkfish
Fly fishing brand

Ruiz+Company
ruizcompany.com
Spain
2006

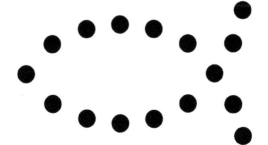

Coral Tech
Super computers

Triboro
triborodesign.com
USA
2000

Belgian Breast Clinic
Aesthetic surgery

Chilli Design & Multimedia
chilli.be
Belgium
2012

Red Herring Real Restaurants
Restaurant & bait bar

Design: Mark Fox
Design Studio: BlackDog
designisplay.com
USA
1999

L'Animal et l'homme
Voluntary association of web
content & creation of events
dedicated to animal intelligence

Policestudio
policestudio.fr
France
2020

A Morsa
Multimedia

Ze Cardoso
zecardoso.com
Portugal
2012

Sardine
FraudTech & compliance

What Else Studio
whatelse.studio
USA
2022

Streamstalkin 24/7 / Olaf Lindner
Fishing courses

Studio Jens Mennicke
jensmennicke.com
Germany
2009

SEM label
Music label

Büro Ink
bueroink.com
France
2013

Fishery Burgas
Import & export of fish products

Stefan Kanchev
stefankanchev.com
Bulgaria
1950–1980

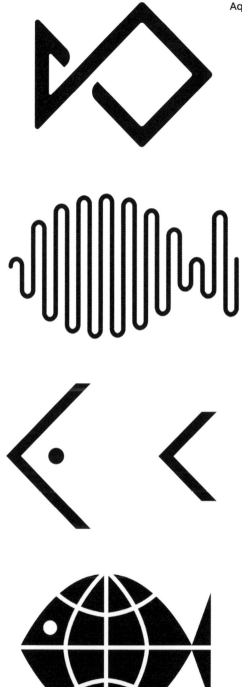

Fish Place
Cajun seafood fast food chain

Design Company: Pentagram
Art Director: DJ Stout
Designer: Barrett Fry
barrettfry.com
USA
2011

Madam Sixty Ate
Restaurant   .

Substance Ltd
substance.hk
Australia
2011

Fosforos del Pirineo
Matchbox factory

Cruz Novillo
cruznovillo.com
Spain
1968

ARCI Lega per l'Ambiente
Environmental association

CS Coopstudio
communicationservices.it
Italy
1983

New Bedford Whaling Museum
Museum

Malcolm Grear Designers
mgrear.com
USA
2000

British Heart Foundation:
The Mending Broken
Hearts Appeal
Charity

Magpie Studio
magpie-studio.com
United Kingdom
2010

Rari Nantes Bogliasco
Swimming & water polo

Sergio Bianco
sergiobianco.it
Italy
1997

Stella Maris
Historical hotel residence

Sergio Bianco
sergiobianco.it
Italy
1998

AlphaFish
Digital investment

Ascend Studio
ascendstudio.co.uk
USA
2014

Fish Central
Fish restaurant

Atelier Works
atelierworks.co.uk
United Kingdom
2006

What's The Catch
Fishmongers

OK Creative Agency
okcreative.agency
United Kingdom
2020

Benito Díaz
Sport fishing shop

David de la Fuente
daviddelafuente.com
Spain
2010

Les Pinces
Lobster restaurant

Policestudio
policestudio.fr
France
2014

This is Pacifica
thisispacifica.com
Portugal
2020

Santiago
TV series

This is Pacifica
thisispacifica.com
Portugal
2022

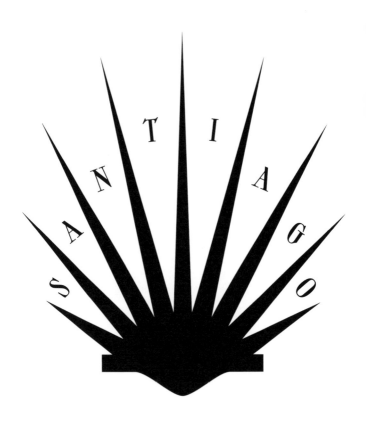

Supple Studio
supple.studio
United Kingdom
2018

Kin Seafood
Seafood

StudioBand®
studioband.com.au
Australia
2022

Twin Fin Rum
Spirit

Buddy
buddycreative.com
United Kingdom
2019

Kettle
3D animation & visual effects

Sam Dallyn
samdallyn.co.uk
United Kingdom
2010

Ljubljanski Sejem
Fair organiser

Edi Berk, KROG
ediberk.com
Slovenia
1994

Twin Fin

RUM

Kettle©

FXU Marine Conservation Group
Fundraising events for Falmouth
& Exeter University students

I See Sea
iseesea.co.uk
United Kingdom
2012

Bears

Solide
Clothing

Arnaud Mercier (Elixirstudio)
arnaud.area17.com
France
2003

Kinoto Studio
kinotostudio.com
Canada
2021

Meg – Modern
Exercise Goods
Cork exercise equipment

Common Kind
commonkind.co.uk
United Kingdom
2019

The Different Toy
Range of toys for House of Fraser

Minale Tattersfield
minaletattersfield.com
United Kingdom
1968

Cerebral Palsy Action (CPA)
Charity

Eggers Diaper
eggers-diaper.com
United Kingdom
1999

Defero
Music

Lee Goater
leegoater.com
United Kingdom
2009

Rocks Manchester
Charity

Fivefootsix
fivefootsix.co.uk
United Kingdom
2012

Aanifeira
Animal rescue association

Atelier d'alves
atelierdalves.com
Portugal
2010

Blue Bear Outside
Technical outdoor
product company

Kelly Sue Webb
& Cardon Webb
kellysuewebb.com
& cardonwebb.com
USA
2012

40

RRB
National rescue service
organisation

Add Studio
addstudio.se
Sweden
2019

City of Berne
Administration of the city

Atelier Bundi
atelierbundi.ch
Switzerland
1985

**Aerzteges–ellschaft des
Kantons Bern (Doctor's
Society of the Canton Berne)**
Doctor's society

Atelier Bundi
atelierbundi.ch
Switzerland
2010

Behr
Paint manufacturer

Academy of Art University
academyart.edu
USA
2010

Bistro Bruno
Restaurant

Anne Angel Designs
angeldesigns.com.au
Australia
2011

3 Bears
The Four Seasons Resort
Whistler

dng studio
dngstudio.com
Canada
2013

Leckerlee Lebkuchen
Bakery

Strohl
strohlsf.com
USA
2011

Fosforos del Pirineo
Matchbox factory

Cruz Novillo
cruznovillo.com
Spain
1968

Cub Studio Ltd
Animation studio

O Street
ostreet.co.uk
United Kingdom
2021

Blesstown Bruins
Ice hockey team

Bless
blessdesign.com
United Kingdom
2008

203
Record label

Mash Creative
mashcreative.co.uk
Finland / USA
2013

Birds

Jansens Geudens
Chicken specialties & caterer

Chilli
Chilli.be
Belgium
2017

Sweet Chick
Premium southern comfort
food restaurant chain

High Tide
hightidenyc.com
USA
2021

Mama Shelter
Hotel

GBH Design
gregorybonnerhale.com
France
2008

Eggs and Poultry
Production of eggs & poultry

Stefan Kanchev
stefankanchev.com
Bulgaria
1950–1980

Aunt Reg's Eggs
Grocery & baked goods

The Hideout
thehideout.design
USA
2020

Primario
Tapas restaurant

Marnich Associates
marnich.com
Spain
2008

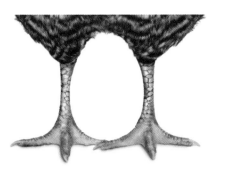

Roost
Co-working space

Tim Boelaars
timboelaars.com
The Netherlands
2016

Bulgarreklama
Advertising

Stefan Kanchev
stefankanchev.com
Bulgaria
1958

Kenkävero
Arts & craft center

Kari Piippo Oy
piippo.com/kari
Finland
1990

Gallus
Wine production

Likovni Studio
list.hr
Croatia
2000

Leon's
Restaurant

Jay Fletcher
jfletcherdesign.com
USA
2014

British Pathé
Media

Bunch
bunchdesign.com
United Kingdom
2011

Moa Brewing
Craft beer

Seachange
Seachange.studio
New Zealand
2020

Käss Food & Pastries
Deli

Bionic Systems
bionic-systems.com
Germany
2008

Era Tutta Campagna
Web agency

Emanuele Abrate
emanueleabrate.com
Italy
2021

Bulgarsko Vezmo
Bulgarian textiles

Stefan Kanchev
stefankanchev.com
Bulgaria
1950–1980

Vision Training North East
Training company

Build
wearebuild.com
United Kingdom
2008

Bright Young Brits
A collective of British
creative talent

Magpie Studio
magpie-studio.com
United Kingdom
2012

Maeve Durnan
Home tutoring for children

Graphical House
graphicalhouse.co.uk
United Kingdom
2011

Online Degree
Education

Brandclay
brandclay.com
USA
2016

Owl Optics
Eyewear brand

Stiletto NYC
stilettonyc.com
Germany
2011

Caboo
Household goods

Abby Haddican Studio
abbyhaddican.com
Canada
2021

Owly
Musical services

Hunch
designbyhunch.com
Argentina
2020

Hardpop
Nightclub

Face
designbyface.com
Mexico
2012

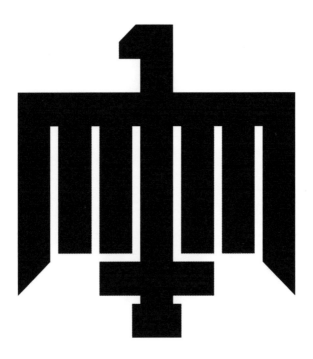

Deutscher Bundestag
German federal parliament

büro uebele visuelle
kommunikation
uebele.com
Germany
2009

Trouble Disco
Event promoter

SleepOp
sleepop.com
USA
2010

Charleston Peace One Day
Organisation promoting
the benefits of peace

Jay Fletcher
jfletcherdesign.com
USA
2009

Perutnina Ptuj
Chicken farm

Edi Berk, KROG
ediberk.com
Slovenia
1983

Ikepod
Luxury watchmaker

Studio Berg
studioberg.com
Switzerland / USA
2006

Teal
Career growth

Order
order.design
USA
2022

Morphic
Products that capture, store
& convert renewable energy

Stockholm Design Lab
stockholmdesignlab.se
Sweden
2008

Tero
Networking solutions

Hunch
designbyhunch.com
Argentina
2020

Ancient Rice
Food produce

Airside Nippon
airside.jp
Japan
2021

Ambaba
Washable nappy company

Graphical House
graphicalhouse.com
United Kingdom
2008

in–d
Film advertising agency

Klor
klor.co.uk
United Kingdom
2006

Bird's of a Feather
Photography collective

Beard is the New Black
beardisthenewblack.com
USA
2010

Feed
Self-initiated

Büro Destruct
burodestruct.net
Switzerland
2020

Dabton House
Luxury private residence

Touch
thetouchagency.co.uk
United Kingdom
2023

Eagle
Aviation

Brandclay
brandclay.com
USA
2016

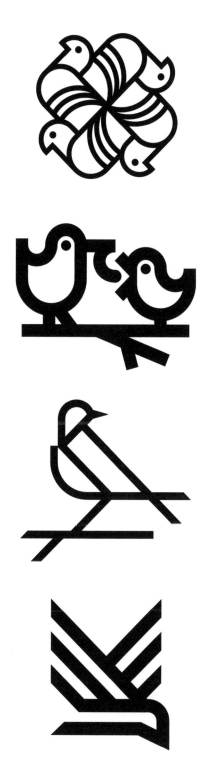

Experiencia Gourmet
Gourmet foodhall

Lewis Moberly
lewismoberly.com
Mexico
2011

Dalaco
Jewellery designers

Believe in®
believein.co.uk
United Kingdom
2012

Messagebird
Omnichannel automation
platform for APIs, service
& marketing

Tim Boelaars
timboelaars.com
The Netherlands
2015

**Association France-Pologne
du Puy-de-Dôme**
Cultural exchange between
France & Poland

Marian Nowinski
nowinski.pl
France
2006

Blackbird
Hospitality technology platform

High Tide
hightidenyc.com
USA
2022

Augusto & Mendonça Alves
Law firm

BRBAUEN
brbauen.com
Brazil
2022

77

United States Institute of Peace
Conflict management center

Malcolm Grear Designers
mgrear.com
USA
1988

American Design Club
Platform for American designers

Studio Lin
studiolin.org
USA
2009

**United States Department
of Health and Human Services**
US government's agency
for protecting health

Malcolm Grear Designers
mgrear.com
USA
1980

**Manomet Center for
Conservation Sciences**
Organisation for conserving
natural resources

Malcolm Grear Designers
mgrear.com
USA
1992

Cross & Corner
Bar & restaurant

Touch
thetouchagency.co.uk
United Kingdom
2013

Sherpa Bird
Travel blog

Birds

Jay Fletcher
jfletcherdesign.com
USA
2012

Vennes
Healthy energy snacks

Cherry Bomb Creative Co
cherrybomb.com.mx
Mexico
2021

Noopii
Baby product company

Ima Creative
imacreative.studio
New Zealand
2019

Randa's Handmade Soaps
Health & beauty products

The Hideout
thehideout.design
USA
2021

United Nations Dove
NGO

dng studio
dngstudio.com
Liberia
2011

Sweet Whistle
Curated gift boxes

High Tide
hightidenyc.com
USA
2016

The Corner House
Hospitality

Touch
thetouchagency.co.uk
United Kingdom
2022

JHA
Energy consultancy

Purpose
purpose.co.uk
United Kingdom
1992

Cardinal Café
Café

Hat-trick Design
hat-trickdesign.co.uk
United Kingdom
2008

SwanSongs
Non-profit musician organisation
that plays requests for individuals
transitioning into death

Macnab Design
macnabdesign.com
USA
1998

The Rashi School
Boston area reform Jewish
day school

Malcolm Grear Designers
mgrear.com
USA
2009

Benedict's B
Home & garden décor

Design Company: BrandsBC
Designer: Dale Nigel Goble
dngstudio.com
Canada
2009

**Evangelisch Lutherse
Gemeente Amsterdam**
Church

Total Identity
totalidentity.com
Holland
2007

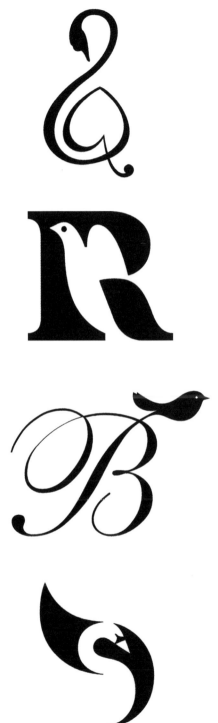

Scotton Consulting
Financial consultants

Chilli Design & Multimedia
chilli.be
Belgium
2012

Penguin
Self-initiated

kissmiklos
kissmiklos.com
Hungary
2020

Cantus Michaelis Choir
Music

Kari Piippo Oy
piippo.com/kari
Finland
1993

TM

&DUCK
Self–initiated

kissmiklos
kissmiklos.com
Hungary
2020

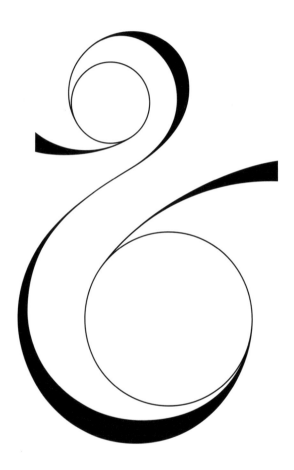

Albatros Turizam
Travel agent

Likovni Studio
list.hr
Croatia
1998

Birds

Welkin Health
Care management software
for healthcare

Fuzzco
fuzzco.com
USA
2016

The Crown Estate
Property management company

DNCO
dnco.com
United Kingdom
2014

Plaid Tag
Clothing line

Jay Fletcher
jfletcherdesign.com
USA
2012

Yukon College Loon
Branding agency /
educational institution

Design Company:
Taiji Brand Group
Design: Dale Nigel Goble
dngstudio.com
Canada
2009

Lucky Duck
Takeaway food

Angel & Anchor
angelandanchor.com
United Kingdom
2022

Gander
takeagander.com
USA
2023

TWO CAN Toucan
Educational books

Minale Tattersfield
minaletattersfield.com
United Kingdom
2002

CeeGee Clothing
Clothing

Mash Creative
mashcreative.co.uk
United Kingdom
2011

Fernweh Bar
Bar

Büro Destruct
burodestruct.net
Switzerland
2022

Bird
Running app

Fuzzco
fuzzco.com
USA
2019

Cats

Lion Playing Cards
Playing card brand

Glad
weareglad.com
2012

Style 18
Clothing

Stefan Kanchev
stefankanchev.com
Bulgaria
1950–1980

Music Saves
Record store

Mikey Burton Design & Illustration
mikeyburton.com
USA
2007

MoonCat Games
Video games publishing

Alexandra Francis
alexandrafrancis.com
United Kingdom
2022

Eveready Battery Co.
Battery manufacturer

Design: Mark Fox
Design Company: BlackDog
(for Landor Associates)
Art Director: Jeff Carino
designisplay.com
USA
1999

Monochromatic Solutions
Interpretation

Sali Tabacchi Inc.
salitabacchi.com
United Kingdom / Spain
2010

Meowoodle
Blog

Skinny Ships
skinnyships.com
USA
2011

The Club
Veterinary

El Paso, Galeria de Comunicación
elpasocomunicacion.com
Spain
2010

**International Film Festival
Rotterdam**
Film festival

75B
75b.nl
Holland
2008

Fosforos del Pirineo
Matchbox factory

Cruz Novillo
cruznovillo.com
Spain
1968

Lion's Feet Media
Publishing

Riley Cran
rileycran.com
United Kingdom
2011

The Red Lion
Disco

Lance Wyman
lancewyman.com
Mexico

Jay Fletcher
jfletcherdesign.com
USA
2012

Custom House Crest
Finance

Taiji Brand Group
& Dale Nigel Goble
dngstudio.com
Canada
2009

LDN
Clothing

Face
designbyface.com
United Kingdom
2012

Kanton Zurich
Department for the canton
Zurich region

Gilbert-Lodge
gilbert-lodge.com
Switzerland
2009

Commune of Haeggenschwil
Council

Alltag
alltag.ch
Switzerland
2012

Momobil
Food takeaway

Büro Destruct
burodestruct.net
Switzerland
2019

Lion
Self–initiated

kissmiklos
kissmiklos.com
Hungary
2019

Triple Co Roast
Coffee roasters

Angel & Anchor
angelandanchor.com
United Kingdom
2021

Natural First
Tea shop

Onion Design Associates
oniondesin.com.tw
Taiwan Province of China
2021

Chingu
Korean restaurant

Frank Norton Studio
frank-norton.com
USA
2023

Sura Noodle Bar
Restaurant

Frank Norton Studio
frank-norton.com
USA
2021

The Blue Tiger Company
Hospitality

Luke Woodhouse
lukewoodhouse.com
United Kingdom
2012

Dogs

MiaCara
Exclusive dog accessories

Atelier 1A
atelier1a.com
Germany
2011

Travis Ladue
travisladue.com
USA
2011

Daily Dog
Pet care vitamins

Date Of Birth
dateofbirth.com.au
Australia
2019

Poochie Amour
eBoutique for dogs

Allies Design Studio
alliesdesign.com
United Kingdom
2005

Defero
Music

Lee Goater
leegoater.com
United Kingdom
2009

Doggy.com
Directory of service providers
for your dog

Dan Fleming Design
danflemingdesign.com
USA
2005

LunaWolf
Production company

Classmate Studio
classmatestudio.com
Hungary / Finland
2023

Pracownia N22
Creative company

Martiszu
martiszu.com
Poland
2012

Wanna
Healthy dog food

Fuzzco
fuzzco.com
USA
2018

Veter
Veterinary Clinic

Enrike Puerto
enrikepuerto.com
Mexico
2021

Beantown Bed & Biscuit
Veterinary care

Bluerock Design
bluerockdesignco.com
USA
2010

Teckel Consulting
HR consulting & coaching

Martiszu
martiszu.com
Poland
2015

Finn
Pet wellness brand

Gander
takeagander.com
USA
2020

Compis
Products for pets

Manifiesto
bymanifiesto.mx
Mexico
2020

Single Exhibition
National fair of singles

Maurizio Milani
milanidesign.it
Italy
1997

Elephants

Mammoth
Mountain resort &
international ski destination

Hornall Anderson (US office)
hornallanderson.com
USA
2008

Any Junk?
Removal company

Bless
blessdesign.com
United Kingdom
2004

Posto Jumbo
Gas station

Miran Design /
Associados Propaganda
mirandesign.daportfolio.com
Brazil
1974

Safari Into Africa
Safari tour operator

Glad
weareglad.com
Zambia
2012

Growcase
Design agency

Riley Cran
rileycran.com
Norway
2011

Heartwork
Art benefit for Target House

Invisible Creature, Inc.
invisiblecreature.com
USA
2011

Guulp
Liquor store

Mariela Mezquita
marielamezquita.com
Mexico
2021

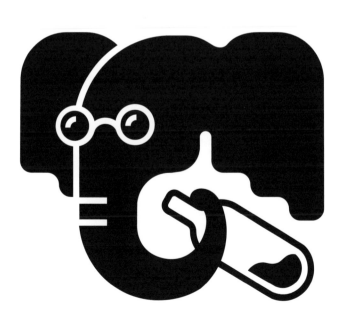

Lightfoot
Driver coaching technology

Buddy
buddycreative.com
United Kingdom
2012

Horses

La Bastide
Country house for kids

Philipp Dornbierer
yehteh.ch
Italy
2013

Reitschule Bern
Cultural center

Büro Destruct
burodestruct.net
Switzerland
2012

It's the Glue
Transformative design

Mikey Burton Design & Illustration
mikeyburton.com
Germany
2013

Black Knight
Printer

Sam Dallyn
samdallyn.co.uk
United Kingdom
2004

Channel 4: 4 Racing
Broadcaster

Magpie Studio
magpie-studio.com
United Kingdom
2012

**Bluewater Shopping Centre
(Lend Lease)**
Shopping centre

Minale Tattersfield
minaletattersfield.com
United Kingdom
1997

Black©

French Express
Music label

Philipp Dornbierer
Yehteh.ch
USA
2009

Northern Horse Park
Horse-themed park

6D
6d-k.com
Japan
2016

Ikuzai
CBD cosmetics

Mubien Brands
mubien.com
Spain
2021

Calhoun's
Restaurant

Jay Fletcher
jfletcherdesign.com
USA
2019

The New Religion
Theatre company

Monnet Design
monnet.ca
Canada
1985

Insects

Cauca
Honey

invade
invade.design
Colombia
2021

Kaposvár Kincse
Municipality of Kaposvár

kissmiklos
kissmiklos.com
Hungary
2018

Hive
Bee-keeping

Mark Weaver
mrkwvr.com
USA
2012

eLearning Industry
eLearning

AG Design Agency
agdesignagency.com
Greece
2020

150

Be Collective
Fashion brand

Ateljé Altmann AB
ateljealtmann.com
United Kingdom
2009

E.G.Flewellen's Bee Farm
Bee-keeping

22°
area-22.com
USA
2012

Plan Bee
Bee-keeping

KVGD Studio
kerrvernon.co.uk
United Kingdom
2012

Quin B Studio
Interior design

Client: Bailey Quin
Design: Jessica Hische
jessicahische.is
USA
2011

Fosforos del Pirineo
Matchbox factory

Cruz Novillo
cruznovillo.com
Spain
1968

Miskeeto
User experience
strategy & design

David Airey
davidairey.com
USA
2007

Papalote
Children's museum

Lance Wyman
lancewyman.com
Mexico

The Transformation Trust
Extracurricular activities
for at-risk school kids

Atelier Works
atelierworks.co.uk
United Kingdom
2015

Liberty for Life
Life coach

John Dowling
wearemucho.com
United Kingdom
2005

Skeeble
Digital App

Vingtneuf Degres
29-degres.com
Switzerland
2011

Butterfly World
Leisure & tourism

Mytton Williams
myttonwilliams.co.uk
United Kingdom
2009

Ciba Pharmaceuticals
Pharmaceuticals

Entro Communications
& Gottschalk + Ash
entro.com
Switzerland
1995

Emerge
Domestic violence support

Frontline Design
frontlinedesign.com.au
Australia
2008

Slow Food
Non-profit organisation

Alessandri Design
alessandri-design.at
Austria
2010

We Compost
Commercial composting

Seachange
Seachange.studio
New Zealand
2019

Celine Roelens – The Goldbeetle
Jewellery designer

Chilli
Chilli.be
Belgium
2018

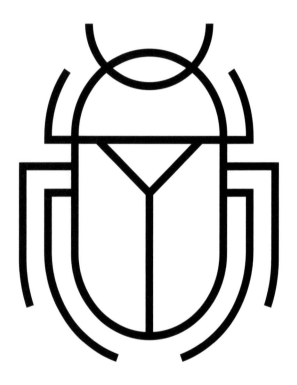

Mythical

Freckle / The Institute of Awesome
Online administrative application

Eight Hour Day
eighthourday.com
USA
2011

Trafford Sword Club
Fencing club

Telling Stories Studio
tellingstories.co.uk
United Kingdom
2012

Borna & Fils
Fashion house

Bunch
bunchdesign.com
France
2012

Prehm & Arendt
Wine distribution

Bionic Systems
bionic-systems.com
Germany
2001

Smith Electric Vehicles
Car manufacturer

Strohl
strohlsf.com
USA
2011

Avion Hotel
Hospitality

UNTZ UNTZ Graphic
Design Studio
untzuntz.pl
Poland
2011

167

Satorisan
Shoes

Koto
koto.studio
Spain
2019

Primates

David Sadaris
Author

Michael Schwab Studio
michaelschwab.com
USA
2008

Kipling
Accessories designer

Base Design
basedesign.com
Belgium
2008

The Kubricks
Music

Mash Creative
mashcreative.co.uk
United Kingdom
2012

Three Drunk Monkeys
Advertising agency

Mark Gowing Design
markgowing.com
Australia
2007

SLS Hotels Hospitality

GBH Design
gregorybonnerhale.com
USA
2008

The Jane
Hospitality

Schwartz & Sons
schwartzandsonsny.com
USA
2010

A.P.E.
Music collective

SleepOp
sleepop.com
USA
2006

Myth Monkey Beer
Craft beer microbrewery

Meat Studio
meat.studio
China / Canada
2019

**Sumatran Orangutan Society
(SOS)**
Conservation charity

Dan Fleming Design
danflemingdesign.com
United Kingdom
2013

Reptiles
&
Amphibians

Pola Honora
Water purification systems

Likovni Studio
list.hr
Croatia
1999

British Medical Association (BMA)
Trade union

Lloyd Northover
Designer: John David Lloyd
& Martin Skeet
lloydnorthover.com
United Kingdom
1995

Farmacia García
Pharmacy

Modesto García
modestogarcia.com
Spain
2006

Clinical Information Advantages Inc.
Computer program

Coco Raynes Associates, Inc.
raynesassociates.com
USA
Late 1980s

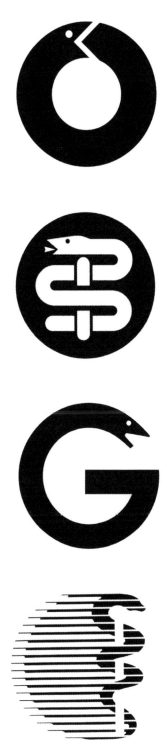

Mediolanum Squash Club
Squash center

Maurizio Milani
milanidesign.it
Italy
1994

Pompei
Archaeology

Studio Lupi
italolupistudio.com
Italy
2001

Figue
Clothing

Schwartz & Sons
schwartzandsonsny.com
USA
2012

BOSSÉ
Night club

Estudio Albino
estudioalbino.com
Mexico
2017

Capital Pecado Cervecería
Craft brewery

Estudio Albino
estudioalbino.com
Mexico
2018

Iconix
Cosmetics

Dan Alexander + Co.
daitd.com
France
2018 – 2019

Snake on Glass
Self–initiated

kissmiklos
kissmiklos.com
Hungary
2018

Total Learning Concepts
Pharmaceutical sales training

Malcolm Grear Designers
mgrear.com
USA
2004

Brekeke
Telephony software company

Hazen Creative
hazencreative.com
USA
2012

LaRana
Clothing center

Maurizio Milani
milanidesign.it
Italy
1983

Plava žaba
Rowing team

Likovni Studio
list.hr
Croatia
2007

De hofleverancier
Shop specialised in ponds
& water features

Chilli
Chilli.be
Belgium
2016

185

The Beach Phi Phi
Exclusive resort

Chilli Design & Multimedia
chilli.be
Thailand
2013

Gundari Resost
Resort

AG Design Agency
agdesignagency.com
Greece
2020

Allay California / TurtleScarf
Clothing & accessories

Hazen Creative
hazencreative.com
USA
2008

Peace Coffee
Beverage

Werner Design Werks
Designers: Abby Haddican
& Sharon Werner
wdw.com
USA
2021

Marwell Wildlife Trust
Wildlife conservation
research trust

Hat-trick Design
hat-trick design.co.uk
United Kingdom
2009

Gecko Kids Ltd.
Clothing

Hazen Creative
hazencreative.com
Mauritius
2011

Claxe
Startup helping online
marketeers & web
entrepreneurs monitor
their competition

Studio de Ronners
deronners.com
The Netherlands
2017

The Crocodile
Rock club & bar

SleepOp
sleepop.com
USA
2009

GECKO

Door No.4
Hospitality / bar

HUMAN
byhuman.mx
Cayman Islands
2020

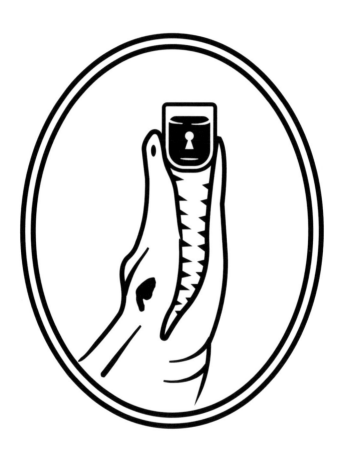

Stags

Hirschbühl
Needlework

Harry Metzler Studio
harrymetzler.com
Austria
1990

Mini McGhee
Luxury Scottish knitwear

Graphical House
graphicalhouse.com
United Kingdom
2013

Deerpath Lookout
Hospitality

dng studio
dngstudio.com
Canada
2009

Buckeye Roadhouse
Restaurant

Client: Real Restaurants
Design: BlackDog
Illustrator: Mark Fox
designisplay.com
USA
1991

Hotel Minho
Hotel & spa

R2
r2design.pt
Portugal
2011

Jackson
Estate agents

Mash Creative & Socio Design
mashcreative.co.uk
& sociodesign.co.uk
United Kingdom
2013

195

**MOME Moholy-Nagy University
of Art and Design Budapest**
University

Balás Design
balasdesign.hu
Hungary
2011

Other

Anthony Dimitre
Illustration & graphic design

Anthony Dimitre
anthonydimitre.com
USA
2010

Fokse
Fundraising association

Maddison Graphic
maddison graphic.com
United Kingdom
2007

Ouou
Online store

Survival Mode
survivalmode.pl
Poland
2012

Hunters Alley
Social app

Strohl
strohlsf.com
USA
2013

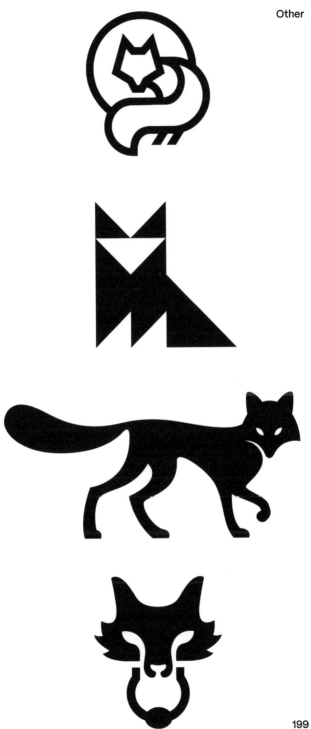

199

Joni
Verjus drink

MAKEBARDO
makebardo.com
USA
2022

Wolf
Children's clothing

Jan en Randoald
janenrandoald.be
Belgium
2010

Squire Fox
Photography

Fuzzco
fuzzco.com
USA
2012

Belk
Plant-based restaurant

Cherry Bomb Creative Co
cherrybomb.com.mx
Dubai
2019

Squirrels
Programme for four to six-
year-old children operated
by The Scout Association

Supple Studio & Rob Clarke
supplestudio.com & robclarke.com
United Kingdom
2021

Downtown Toronto Pipe Club
Pipe lovers' organisation

Jay Fletcher
jfletcherdesign.com
Canada
2013

Well Fired Pizza
Food

Angel & Anchor
angelandanchor.com
United Kingdom
2023

Convoy
Design agency

Convoy
convoyinteractive.com
Germany
2003

Buffalo Systems
Extreme outdoor clothing

The Consult
theconsult.com
United Kingdom
2012

Barsa
Spanish tapas restaurant

Fuzzco
fuzzco.com
USA
2010

Merrill Lynch
Finance

King-Casey
king-casey.com
USA
1971

Steven Stewart
Business consultancy

Mike Collinge
mikecollinge.com
New Zealand
2012

Milkraft
Paper manufacturers

COMMUNE
commune-inc.jp
Japan
2009

Cubby's Chicago Beef
Restaurant

Kelly Sue Webb & Cardon Webb
kellysuewebb.com
& cardonwebb.com
USA
2012

Angry Badgers
Football club

Tim Fellowes
United Kingdom
2010

White Mausu
Asian-inspired condiments

Revert Design
revertdesign.net
Ireland
2017

Halo Safet
Catering

Armada Brand Service Studio
armada.si
Slovenia
2007

The Pink Pig
Bakery & restaurant

Design Company: Pentagram
Design Art Director: DJ Stout
Designer: Barrett Fry
barrettfry.com
USA
2012

The Ginger Pig
Butchers

Allies Design Studio
alliesdesign.com
United Kingdom
2007

Olive Pork
Premium pork products

Brandlab
brandlab.ie
Ireland
2020

Gemeinde Rechberghausen
A town in the district of Göppingen
in Baden-Württemberg in southern
Germany

büro uebele visuelle kommunikation
uebele.com
Germany
2004

Deer
Hospitality

dng studio
dngstudio.com
Canada
2013

Minnesota Zoo
Zoo

Lance Wyman
lancewyman.com
USA

Dig Inn
Restaurant chain

High Tide
hightidenyc.com
USA
2015

O'Hare Electric
Electric service

Brandclay
brandclay.com
USA
2018

Fair to Midland
Bar & restaurant

Frank Norton Studio
frank-norton.com
USA
2021

Nexcite
Performance-enhancing drink

Amore
amore.se
Sweden
2005

Fast Rabbit
Sportswear for children

Miran Design
mirandesign.daportfolio.com
Brazil
1995

18 Rabbits Granola
Producer of granola bars

Strohl
strohlsf.com
USA
2007

The Wool Pot
Sustainable product design /
gardening / horticulture

Seachange
Seachange.studio
New Zealand
2022

New Kid Coffee Roasters
Coffee roasters

Angel & Anchor
angelandanchor.com
Ireland
2023

Kyle Poff Design Inc.
Graphic design

Kyle Poff Design Inc.
krop.com/kylepoff
USA
2011

The Baby Goat Co
Sports backpacks

Enrique Puerto
enrikepuerto.com
Colombia
2021

Blackbelly
Restaurant

Berger & Föhr
bergerfohr.com
USA
2014

Tourism Australia
Tourism industry

Interbrand
interbrand.com
Australia
2012

Raymond Farquhar
Architectural studio

Reghardt
reghardt.com
United Kingdom
2011

Two Giraffes
Web development

Brandclay
brandclay.com
USA
2011

Express Card
PC cards

Leader Creative
leadercreative.com
USA
2005

giraffe

Victor Russo's Osteria
Restaurant

Total Identity
totalidentity.com
Holland
2010

Line of Life Project for Suntory
Manufacture and sale of alcoholic
beverages & soft drinks

6D
6d-k.com
Japan
2016

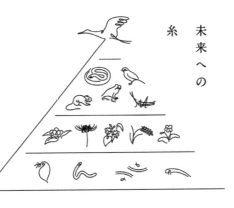

Animal Logo
Compiled & published
by Counter-Print
counter-print.co.uk

Design:
Counter-Print

First published in 2013.
Reprinted in 2014, 2015.

This revised and expanded
edition published in 2024.
Reprinted in 2024.

Printed by 1010 Printing
International Ltd, China

© Counter-Print 2024

ISBN:
978-0-9570816-1-1

With special thanks to all the
contributors for their support,
time and talent.

Cover Logos Left to Right:
Veter by Enrike Puerto,
We Compost by Seachange,
De hofleverancier by Chilli,
The Red Lion by Lance Wyman,
Feed by Büro Destruct,
MoonCat Games
by Alexandra Francis,
Deutscher Bundestag
by büro uebele visuelle,
Claxe by Studio de Ronners,
What's The Catch by
OK Creative Agency.

Spine Logos Top to Bottom:
Roost by Tim Boelaars,
International Film Festival
Rotterdam by 75B,
Cub Studio Ltd by O Street.